75

D0508361

Your Kids
and the
OCCULT

Johanna
Michaelsen

HARVEST HOUSE PUBLISHERS
Eugene, Oregon 97402

YOUR KIDS AND THE OCCULT

Taken from **LIKE LAMBS TO THE SLAUGHTER**
Copyright © 1989 by Johanna Michaelsen
Published by Harvest House Publishers
Eugene, Oregon 97402

ISBN 0-89081-804-5

Printed in the United States of America.

INTRODUCTION

New Year's Eve, 1983. I was sitting in the wings of Trinity Broadcasting Network wondering what on earth I was going to say. Hal Lindsey was hosting the New Year's television special and had asked me to discuss the most significant developments in the occult during the past year. Actually it had been a fairly quiet year on the occult scene. And yet I had the feeling that there was something tremendously important that I was supposed to say that night about the occult. "Please, Lord," I fervently prayed, "what is it that You want me to talk about?" A few moments of silence . . . and then I heard it—a still, small voice that said, "Look what they're doing to My children." And then again, "*Look what they're doing to My children!*"

As Hal and I discussed the occult, I talked about a Smurfs' cartoon I had watched a few weeks before in which the evil Gargamel had been given directions to "draw a circle in the ground, and in that circle draw a pentagram . . ."—thereby teaching millions of tiny fans the basics of ritual magic. And I mentioned that schools across the country were being inundated with occult books, assignments, and manuals.

After the program I was told that the phone lines of TBN were jammed for several hours with parents wanting to know more about how their kids were being lured and programmed into the occult and what they could do to counteract the trend.

New Age Voices

It is truly ironic that our space-age, technological civilization whose god has been science, progress, rationalism, and cold-blooded empiricism has seen a mass stampede in the direction of Eastern mysticism and occultism that constitutes the backbone of the New Age Movement.

The statistics are staggering. According to a poll conducted by George Gallup, Jr., at least one out of every four Americans now believes in reincarnation.[1] In a recent poll by the University of Chicago's National Opinion Research Council (NORC), two million Americans report that they've had out-of-body experiences or near-death experiences.[2] Over 20 million are tuning into psychics and channelers. Almost half of American adults (42 percent) now believe they've been in contact with someone who has died. And at least two-thirds of these adults report having experienced ESP.

Programming Kids into the Occult

The children have by no means been left untouched or ignored by the spiritual "transformation" of their elders. The children, in fact, are the key targets. It is, after all, the little ones who will be the leaders, teachers, politicians, lawmakers, and parents of tomorrow. What they are taught today as young children about who or what God is and about who they are, what the nature of reality is, what happens to a person after death, and what morality and ethics are based on must necessarily have a tremendous impact on the direction the society of the future will take. It is staggering to realize to what extent the answers they are developing to these crucial questions are firmly entrenched in occult philosophy.

The key manipulators of the New Age know that unless you train up and harness the spiritual direction of the children, there will be no New Age. At every level the child's worldview—that is, what he unquestioningly assumes to be true about himself and the world around him—is carefully being molded and programmed.

In growing numbers of schools around the country, the children are being taught how to contact their spirit guides (euphemistically called their "Higher Self" or their "Inner Wisdom") to help them solve problems. They are being sent home with assignments to research their astrological sign or to draw a mandala for art class.

In Gifted-and-Talented programs children are given projects dealing with Ouija boards—how to build them and use them, how to read palms, and how to be like the "amazing Mrs. Hughes," who helps policemen find missing bodies. They are being taught Yoga and meditation and techniques of guided imagery/visualization long used by shamans, mediums, and other occultists. Despite overwhelming documentation of suicides and murders associated with it, Dungeons and Dragons now has a special edition of their "game" especially designed for use in school.

At the movies children are learning that "God" is a "Force" that they can tap into and manipulate for "good" or "evil" depending on their mood. They are learning to control and harness that awesome power through ancient Eastern techniques of mind control. They see that even though "They're ba-a-ck," the evil poltergeists can be defeated through the techniques, chants, and powers of the shaman or the medium.

Saturday-morning cartoons are proving to toddlers that *"I am the power!"* They are told that there are "good" sorceresses and Witches and shamans and wizards who have access to untold power, and that telepathy and telekinesis (and those words are the exact ones used) are normal and useful abilities to cultivate.

To some people these examples may seem thoroughly harmless. "After all," someone said to me once, "I've been watching 'Casper the Friendly Ghost' and 'Bewitched' for years and it never did anything awful to me!" Maybe not, although I believe that such a conclusion is debatable. However, taken in the context of the development and rapid expansion of the New Age Movement, He-Man and the Smurfs suddenly take on a whole new ominous significance.

Because space is limited in a booklet of this size, *Your Kids and the Occult* focuses on those inroads of occult influence over which you as a parent have the most direct control: the types of movies and television shows your children watch, the games and toys they play with, and the way your family celebrates Halloween. But having been alerted to the dangers lurking close to home, it is my hope that many of you will refer to *Like Lambs to the Slaughter* to learn more about the massive indoctrination into occultism and New Age thinking going on in our schools today.

1

The War for Your Child's Mind

Imitation is natural to man from childhood . . . he is the most imitative creature in the world, and learns at first by imitation.[1]

—Aristotle

Train up a child in the way he should go, and when he is old he will not depart from it.

—Proverbs 22:6 (KJV).

The ancient demon gods still live. The gods and goddesses of the Greeks and Romans still rule. The ancient magical symbols, tools, beliefs, and rites hold sway among us yet, absorbed and learned and practiced by eager young apprentices—not in the halls of marbled temples, or in sacred groves, or in a sorcerer's dungeon, but in local movie theaters and living rooms of homes around the country.

From four to seven hours a day, day after day, year after year, our little ones sit transfixed before the phosphorescent altar of their gods, eagerly soaking into the very depths of their beings the lessons and images of violence, occultism, sex, death, and hedonism so powerfully

7

presented to them. Not surprisingly, it's the preschoolers who spend the most time of all glued to the screen.[2] By the time the average American child reaches the age of 18, he will have logged from 15 to 22 thousand hours of television. That works out to a staggering equivalent of ten years of 40-hour weeks![3]

What on earth is a child learning during those hours? More to the point, does it really matter? To suggest that there is something sinister about watching the Smurfs and He-Man and playing with adorable rainbow-colored unicorns is definitely to risk losing one's credibility with many parents and others who simply cannot see anything wrong with them, and who in fact may view them as important developmental tools in a child's life.

And yet it is a fact that many of today's cartoons and toys are saturated not only with violence, but with hard-core occultism, some of it obvious and some of it subtle, but all of it powerful in its potential impact on vulnerable children.

New Agers won't have a difficult time at all explaining to these children the profoundly occult concept of building the Rainbow Bridge (called the *Antahkarana*) between man and the "over soul" who is Lucifer,[4] because these children already know that rainbows are the bridge on which they travel to reach Rainbow Brite, who "has the power of the rainbow to make you happy!" A lot of children won't have a hard time at all accepting the occult belief in the power of crystals, because for years they watched the little dream fairies on "My Little Pony 'N Friends" use crystals to gain power over the evil Night Mare.[5] They will be familiar with the concepts of ESP, because when He-Man suddenly realized he could hear a creature's thoughts, he understood that the creature was talking with his mind. "It's called telepathy," he explained to the millions of children watching.[6] Little girls won't have any problem at all accepting the concept of the Mother Goddess or that they themselves can become goddesses, because for years they lived the fantasy of Wonder Woman and of She-Ra, Princess of Power.

She-Ra

A few days ago my husband, Randolph, and I were in Toys R Us scouting through the aisles to see what was new. All of a sudden I heard a high-pitched little voice crying "SHE-RA! SHE-RA!" The voice belonged to a beautiful little three-year-old boy who was sitting in a shopping cart. He was holding a gray plastic sword from the She-Ra collection and raising it high in the air, even as She-Ra does in the popular cartoon series of that name. "SHE-RA!" he cried again in obvious delight. "I see he's into She-Ra," I observed to the rather red-faced father standing by the boy. "Does he like to watch her on TV?" "Actually, we don't allow him to watch cartoons at all," the father replied. "But all his little friends in our apartment complex do. He learned about She-Ra from them."

Take She-Ra's name, for starters. *Ra* was the name of the ancient Egyptian sun god, and one of the early names of the Mother Goddess,[7] who is worshiped today by thousands of Witches and Neo-pagans. Furthermore, either the writers of "She-Ra" are profoundly knowledgeable of ancient Hermetic lore or else they stumbled upon a remarkable coincidence when they named She-Ra's steed "Spirit." According to the *Book of Lambspring* (1625), a rare Hermetic tract, "the unicorn will be (i.e., represents) the *spirit* at all times. . . ."[8] When the Princess Adora (as in "adore: to worship with profound reverence; to honor or to pay divine honor to; to regard with the utmost devotion, esteem, love, and respect . . .")[9] raises her sword and cries out "For the honor of Greyskull!" she becomes She-Ra as a serpentine stream of energy swirls around her. She then directs the energy beam from the crystal in her sword toward the crystal embedded in Spirit's headdress, and Spirit becomes "Swift Wind," a winged unicorn.

Innocent Unicorn?

The myth of the unicorn probably originated in ancient Babylon. It has generally been regarded as a symbol of purity, despite the fact that ancient legends ascribe to it some decidedly impure and unvirginal activities. It is seen as a symbol of opposites, rather like the *yin/yang*, a combination and androgynous blending of masculine and feminine, which makes it the perfect symbol for the gay and feminist movement of today. New Agers have, in fact, adopted the unicorn as one of their major symbols, viewing it as "the spark of divine light in the darkness of matter and evil,"[10] and as a symbol of the great world leader whom they expect to bring peace on the earth in the New Age. The Bible identifies this leader as the Antichrist, the little horn that rises in the midst of the ten horns which Daniel saw in his vision (Daniel 7:8).

The Crystal Castle

On occasion She-Ra goes to the Crystal Castle to speak to "Light Hope,"[11] a beam of radiant light that speaks to her in a deep, Godlike voice. Light Hope is always seen emanating from the middle of a large triangle on the ground. Around the triangle is a large circle. In ritual magic, the circle is a symbol of protection or containment. Everything inside the circle is safe and protected from the intrusion of any evil or demonic beings. The circle is an ancient symbol for God, as it is timeless, without beginning or end. The triangle (a representation of the Trinity), when placed within the circle, becomes a Thaumaturgic (magic) Triangle, one of the most powerful occult symbols in ritual magic for the conjuration of demons. But all this is contained within the Crystal Castle, and crystal is a symbol for spirit and purity.[12] The message seems clear enough: To She-Ra, the hope for the world is the "Light" which rises forth from their occultic circle. Most New Agers would readily recognize that "Light" as "Lucifer" the lightbearer, whom they believe to be the only hope for the salvation of the world. The final punch line comes at the end of every

She-Ra program in a memorable little ditty: "For the honor of love, we have the power. So can you."

This isn't "just fantasy." Nor is it simply part of the "magic" of childhood. It is heavy-duty, highly sophisticated religious indoctrination disguised as innocent entertainment!

May the Force Be with Who?

Who among us has not seen *Star Wars*, *The Empire Strikes Back*, and *Return of the Jedi*? As spectacularly entertaining and exciting as the trilogy was, George Lucas (according to his biographer, Dale Pollock) was determined to do more with his films than "just entertain."[13] He wanted to create "a modern fairy tale," a "timeless fable" for America and the world. As Lucas said, "I wanted to make a kids film that would strengthen contemporary mythology and introduce a kind of basic morality. . . . Nobody's saying the very basic things; . . . everybody's forgetting to tell the kids, 'Hey, this is right and this is wrong.' " As Pollock observes, "Lucas was imposing his values on the rest of the world, but he felt they were the right values."[14]

Pollock candidly and unequivocally states that "the message of Star Wars is religious. . . . *Lucas wanted to instill in children a belief in a supreme being—not a religious god, but a universal deity that he named the Force, a cosmic energy source that incorporates and consumes all living things*."[15] According to Pollock, Lucas based much of his concept of the Force on the works of author/sorcerer Carlos

Castaneda, who wrote about his experiences with a Mexican Indian sorcerer named Don Juan.

Your Kid the Magician/Warrior

Pollock points out that in the trilogy "Jedi knights are trained to tap into this collective energy, which gives them the status of magician/warrior."[16] To use the Force was to put aside objective reasoning. Both Ben Kenobi and Yoda, whose entire philosophy was Buddhist,[17] repeatedly instructed Luke to "let go of your conscious self . . . act on instinct . . . stretch out with your feelings . . . trust your feelings!"

Using the Force, Ben can hypnotize an Empire warrior and pithily observe that "the Force can have a strong influence on the weak-minded." Using the Force, Yoda can levitate Luke's fighter plane out of the murky swamp. "I don't believe it!" exclaims an awed Skywalker. "That," responds Yoda, "is why you fail."

Put aside all critical faculties, enter an altered state of consciousness, have faith in your faith, and allow the Force to work through you. Nothing shall be withheld from you if only you believe! Herein lies the basis of all occult power. This is how channelers become channelers, how occultists develop occult power, and how millions of our schoolchildren become open to demonic beings.

How many millions of children have yearned to become Jedi knights like Luke Skywalker? How many millions accepted the occultic lessons presented by Yoda and Ben Kenobi, and have incorporated those lessons into the basic framework of their personalities? Their newly implanted yearning to become magician/warriors like their hero, Luke, was fed by the deluge of Star Wars paraphernalia that hit the market after each episode. There were *thousands* of objects to choose from—everything from Star Wars school supplies and lunch pails to Darth Vader pajamas and belt buckles and Princess Lea bubble bath. So many people were collecting Star Wars paraphernalia that in 1986 someone published *The Official Price Guide to Star Trek and Star Wars Collectibles*, which contains "4000 all-new listings!"[18]

Promotional material for "Star Wars Action Figures" was mailed to children in households across the country by Kenner Products. Along with a handsome Star Wars poster, each "Young Jedi Knight" received what seemed to be a personal letter from Luke Skywalker himself, telling about his exciting adventures, even though he "had yet to learn to harness the mystical powers of the Force." At the close of the letter he encourages the children to "be sure to study hard as I did, and May the Force Be With You!"

And need we say there were cartoon series' based on the pugnacious little teddy bear Ewok warriors and on the adventures of the two "Droids," Artoo-Detoo, and See-Threepio.

The Droids didn't seem to last too long, but the Ewoks were popular enough to merit two television movies of their very own. Of course, their tribal shaman always played a prominent part.

"Brave Star" is another one of several cartoon series that have featured shamans in recent years. Brave Star is a handsome intergalactic marshal on a distant planet still going through its Old West phase. Brave Star can call on supernatural powers. By entering an altered state, he can summon to himself the "eyes of a hawk ... the strength of a bear ... the speed of a puma...." When he is in need of special wisdom, he always consults the wise old shaman who trained Brave Star even from his boyhood in the ancient ways.

Smurfed Up

Then of course there are always the Smurfs. Those eternally blue little critters have been Smurfing around now since September of 1981[19] and show no sign of calling it quits. The six-through 11-year-olds made it NBC's number one runaway hit in its first season, breaking all kinds of Nielsen records for Saturday morning viewing. And kids still love the Smurfs. Unlike so much of the violent, loud, scary stuff, kids can identify with the little Smurfs, whose names—Lazy Smurf, Brainy Smurf, Clumsy Smurf, Grumpy Smurf—strike a deep chord of recognition in a lot of little guys!

The little Smurfs spend much of their time avoiding the evil plots of the sinister, wicked, and ever-incompetent sorcerer named Gargamel and his moth-eaten feline familiar, Azariel. Gargamel's chief ambition in life is to capture a Smurf—it seems he likes to eat them. But Papa Smurf is himself a powerful wizard of no small means, and can always be counted on to come to the rescue with the aid of his magic books, spells, amulets, and incantations.

The other reason Gargamel wants to catch Smurfs is to prove to all the other wizards that Smurfs do indeed exist. The other wizards have been ribbing him about it unmercifully. Now, to add insult to injury, Gargamel has just been informed that neither he nor his imaginary Smurfs were invited to the great wizard convention that year. But Gargamel is determined to vindicate himself. He goes into his room and bows low before the "Great Book of Spells" which stands enshrined between two candles. The book has a five-pointed star on the cover. Gargamel calculates that the moon is in just the right phase for him to ask the spirit of the Great Book for a wish, so he conjures him forth.

"Speak the incantation, oh rude one!" commands the irritated voice that issues forth from the pages of the now-open book. Gargamel does so and tells the spirit that he wants him to give him the biggest bird on earth so he can swoop down and capture a Smurf to take to the wizard convention. So the spirit gives him detailed instructions, which include the following: "*Draw a pentagram on the ground.*" There is also some inane incantation along the lines of "Draw this circle on the dirt and sprinkle skunk juice on your shirt!" Gargamel does as he is told, and sure enough, the biggest bird in the world suddenly appears before him: an ostrich! The bird proves totally useless in catching Smurfs, of course, and once again Gargamel is left in stark defeat and humiliation with even the spirit of his own magic book of spells calling him a "bumbling fool neophyte."

True enough! Nevertheless, the point is that the basic procedure for the invocation of spirits used by ritual magicians is pretty much all there, right down to the term "pentagram." The pentagram is a five-pointed star considered to be one of the most powerful tools of conjuration in magical rites. The pentagram with one point upward is used by Witches and other Neo-pagans as a symbol of man and of the divine power he has over the universe.[20] In medieval days it supposedly represented the five wounds of Christ, and as such was used as a charm to keep evil spirits away. Some ritual magicians today still use it in this context to repel evil, and, at least in medieval days, many magicians sewed the pentagram on their robes for protection. When the pentagram is reversed it becomes a symbol of Satan and darkness, and therefore attracts those very forces. With two points up, the pentagram signifies the supposed victory of man and Satan over the Trinity. Keep your eyes open as you watch these kiddie shows; the pentagram, including the satanic inverted version, shows up on a regular basis.

New Age leaders have made it abundantly clear that they are determined to initiate our children into their program. Occult cartoons, stories, movies, toys, games, and comics are to the New Age religion what Sunday school and Bible stories are to Christianity, only multiplied a thousandfold. Apart from the psychological conditioning and desensitizing to occultism brought about by chronic viewing of cartoons and movies like the ones we've been discussing, there are also very real spiritual dangers. The more that children are encouraged to experiment and play with the occult, the more that many of them are going to attract literal demonic beings to themselves. If you think that somehow children are spared from demonic attention simply because they are young and "just playing," you're dead wrong. Satan and his demons are the ultimate legalists; they don't care how old a human being is when he trespasses into demonic territory, and there are numerous well-documented cases of demon possession of children, not the least impressive of which are found in the New Testament.[21]

Violent Report

Not only are children being exposed to occultic influence through the media, but they are also absorbing the violence of our society.[22] A close look at the entertainment available to our children today should give us serious pause. If our children grow up with violence and occultism, then those are the traits and beliefs they will surely reflect to one degree or another in adulthood.

It seems that promoting war and violence is extremely profitable to the toy companies. In 1985 they sold over 1.2 *billion* dollars worth of war toys and accessories! And the toy companies now finance about 85 percent of the cartoon programming.[23]

According to a recent government study, children start imitating what they see on television as early as 14 months of age![24] It seems that a baby of that age can remember how a toy was manipulated on television and a day later repeat those actions when given the toy. Andrew Meltzoff, a psychologist at the University of Washington, concluded that "television may influence early development of speech, language and social skills more than has been thought."[25]

A Full-Time Challenge

There is probably no more challenging, difficult, or rewarding job in the world today than that of raising balanced, healthy, normal, confident, loving, and godly children to become balanced, healthy, normal, confident, loving, and godly adults.

The fact is, you cannot altogether isolate your child from the world. Sooner or later, even the most shielded child is going to find himself exposed to the occult principles that permeate today's society.

While you simply cannot isolate your child forever, neither can you allow him to become steeped in the deeply occultic and mystical principles, fear, and violence presented on virtually every cartoon show and children's program at one time or another—not to mention the rest of what's on television that a lot of children watch along with their parents! Many of these programs, as we have seen, have a very specific message that they want to get across. The trick is to spot that message and not allow it to indoctrinate you or your children! There are a few simple ways to do this.

How to Spot the Message

1. First of all, learn as much as you can about the New Age from a Christian perspective. There are many excellent books on the market to choose from. You don't necessarily need to become an expert on the subject, but you cannot afford to be ignorant of the basic concepts and symbols used to indoctrinate the unwary. You've got to study!

2. Never allow your preschooler to watch television by himself. Even "Sesame Street" has been known to scare the diapers off some little tykes from time to time. Studies conducted by Piaget and others indicate that a child under seven sometimes has a tough time distinguishing fantasy from reality. To him, what happens on that television or movie screen is actually real! Pretty scary if you think about it!

3. Be sure to monitor what your child watches. Author Michael R. Kelley in his excellent book *A Parent's Guide to Television: Making the Most of It* says that ideally a preschool child should never watch action-adventure cartoons that routinely present violent and aggressive behavior, action-adventure dramas, highly violent movies, medical documentaries, soap operas, or the evening news.[26] I would add to that "never" list any show that carries occult themes. These present images that a little one may not be able to handle

for years, and which can become a source of nightmares and excessively fearful or aggressive behavior. Shows like "Winnie the Pooh" and the "Muppet Babies" are generally good ones to stick with. If you're there watching with him, you can talk over what he sees and help him work out anything that may frighten or confuse him.

4. Researchers also suggest that you never allow preschoolers to watch more than one hour of television a day. Television is definitely addictive, and the more TV a child watches when very young, the harder it is to break that addiction. More important, it steals away precious time that could be spent doing something creative. Spend more time playing together or encouraging him to draw, or else read a story. There are some wonderful new storybooks on the market.[27] Consider *The Rumpoles and The Barleys*, by Karen Mezek; Dave Hunt has written a fun new children's story called *The Money Tree*. There's *Bedtime Hugs for Little Ones* by Debby Boone and *Growing Up With Jesus* by Gilbert Beers. Dr. Beers has also written a book called *Parents: Talk With Your Children* that I think has some tremendously valuable insights for parents today.

5. Begin training your little ones to discern the difference between fantasy and reality at an early age. If you tell your child that Santa Claus really lives in the North Pole and that he and his reindeer actually come down the chimney on Christmas Eve, you've lied to him. If you let him think that the Easter bunny is what Resurrection

Sunday is all about, and that the bunny actually comes and hides eggs, you've lied to him. Eventually he's going to figure that out, and then he's entirely likely to conclude that what you told him about Jesus is all just a lie too. It's a wonderful thing for a child to play "let's pretend," but you must help him understand that his pretend play is *not* reality. He is simply not going to be able to fly like Superman out of his second-story window just because he put on a little Superman cape!

6. As your children grow older, teach them what to look for. Rather than totally censoring all questionable reading and viewing material, use that material to help teach them discernment. By the time a child is about 11 or 12, he is generally able to reason more abstractly, and you'll be able to reason things through with him on a level that would have been lost on him at an earlier age. Teach him the difference between the genuine miracles that God performs and the occult counterfeits seen in the movies and cartoons. It's important that your child understands that occult powers can indeed be very real, but that God has repeatedly warned us to stay away from them. Tell your child about Moses and the magicians in Pharaoh's court. Tell him about Joseph and Daniel and Elisha. God, in accordance with His own will and purpose, worked awesome miracles through these men, putting all the occultists, wizards, and sorcerers to shame. You might be surprised at just how discerning a child can be if you give him the tools to work with!

7. Be aware that your exercise of discernment should apply equally to Christian materials as well. For example, the fantasy works of Tolkien and C.S. Lewis reflect an essentially Christian worldview, but they include enough references in their writings to "good" Witches, wizards, and magicians to confuse the average child.

I'm not sure I'm prepared to burn all the little hobbits at the stake, but, as with other fairy tales that present any form of occultism in a positive light, I would certainly exercise caution and make sure that my child was old enough to appreciate the story while still understanding that neither C.S. Lewis nor Tolkien were infallible.[28]

8. Above all, teach your children how to test what they see and hear against the Scripture, for this is God's yardstick for truth.

God has given you the responsibility to raise your children in the way in which they should go. The wisdom of man tells us that belief in the occult is good for children. God, on the other hand, warns us to stay away from the occult at all costs! It's up to you whose advice you choose to follow in the raising of your children.

2

"Pure" Fantasy?

Not everyone agrees that fantasizing about violence and the occult is bad for a kid. Gary Gygax, for example, inventor of the wildly popular and shockingly violent and occultic role-playing game called Dungeons and Dragons (or D & D, as it is commonly known) denies that his "game" has caused anyone to become violent or antisocial. On the contrary, he cites letters from parents who praise the game for helping encourage their children to think, reason, use their imaginations, pursue reading, and even overcome learning disabilities. "People have a need to fantasize. It's a mundane world, it's nice to have something imaginary."[1]

Most assuredly, Fantasy Role Playing (FRP) games, and there are from 350 to 400 different ones out on the market now, do encourage the use of the imagination. Imagination is indeed a wonderful thing. So is fantasy, and I believe that both are a gift from God. And yet both fantasy and imagination have been perverted when used to indulge in and promote practices and beliefs that God has repeatedly and consistently labeled abomination all through Scripture.

The FRP game is played primarily in the minds of the players who, on the basis of the roll of dice, select a character whose role they will play in the game. The players generally find themselves in a medieval world of "swords and sorcery," in search of adventure, treasure, and above all, power—especially supernatural power. The point of the game is to make it through the dungeons, to slash or conjure your way past the monsters, dragons, and whatever . . . or whoever . . . gets in your way, in order to achieve your goals, preferably without getting your character killed off. Of course, should your character get killed, all is not necessarily lost! "Even death loses much of its sting, for often the character can be resurrected or reincarnated."[2] In the case of D & D, the game is controlled by the Dungeon Master, a player who is expected to be committed and brilliant enough to design the unbelievably complex fantasy worlds and adventures of the game, and who in essence gets to play "God," deciding by the roll of dice what goes on in the game.

"Swords and sorcery best describes what this game is all about, for those are the two key fantasy ingredients," says Gygax.[3] In other words, to really get into the spirit of this game, you've got to be into violence, magic, and Witchcraft. The degree and kind of violence in these games doubtlessly stems from the fact that they developed from war games based on historical battles. Many of the FRP games go far beyond the old models in the unbridled sadism and sexual violence (including sodomy, rape, homosexuality, bestiality, and other perversions) which can be vicariously indulged in by the players through their characters. Points are given for varying degrees of mutilation inflicted on a victim or adversary during battles and confrontations. Those whose character is in the category of assassin are instructed in the careful planning and execution of the murder of their victims.[4]

The Occult Element

However, it's the occult element that really makes today's Fantasy Role Playing games so enormously appealing. Dungeons and Dragons, the granddaddy of them all, is based on Tolkien's famed "Ring Trilogy," and has adopted a similar theme and feel. Some of the most important weapons available to the characters in their quest are spells, incantations, conjurations, and magical rituals and practices, many of which have been taken directly from black magic, Witchcraft, Voodoo, and Satanism. From what I can see, there's probably not a form or practice of occultism or devil worship that has not been included somewhere in these "games." The spells must be carefully studied and memorized, and "as with all other types of spells... must be spoken or read aloud."[5] Gygax insists that his work is just a game... a work of pure fantasy... not real—and yet on page 115 of the *Official Advanced Dungeons & Dragons Dungeon Masters Guide*, 1979 edition, under "Spell Research," Gygax advises that "it is absolutely mandatory for the researcher to be of sound mind and body and to have privacy and seclusion free from interruption during the course of his or her spell study. . . . It requires about 8 hours per day of work. . . . Once you have the details of the spell, compare and contrast it with and to existing spells in order to determine its level and any modifications and additions you find necessary in order to have it conform to 'known' magic principles."

Devotees of the games may protest that they're not really casting spells; it's all just fantasy. Yet once again it bears repeating that the participants are nevertheless saturating themselves with the contemplation, study, and promotion of things which the God of the Bible has repeatedly condemned as abomination! (Deuteronomy 18:9ff.). God hates the practice of every form of idolatry and occultism in the real world. Human sacrifice, divination, Witchcraft, superstitions, sorcery, ritual magic, mediumship, spiritism, and necromancy are all flatly condemned by the Word of God. So what makes you think He's going to approve of it in the world of your imagination?

Dr. Thomas Radecki, a consistent and adamant critic of D & D, has stated that the game is "essentially a worship of violence. . . . It's a very intense war game. . . . It's very fascinating. It's a game of fun. But when you have fun with murder, that's dangerous. When you make a game out of war, that's harmful. The game is full of human sacrifice, eating babies, drinking blood, rape, murder of every variety, curses of insanity. It's just a very violent game."[6]

Today there are well over four million players, mostly young males ranging from 8 to 27 years old, who have accepted Mr. Gygax's invitation to enter into that fantasy dream world of sorcery and swords.

One of the recognized dangers inherent in the game is the potential for overidentification with the characters. Reality distortion can occur as some players begin to develop their fantasy character as an alter ego, and some youngsters insist on being called by their character's name. Others have found themselves actually carrying out the rapes, robberies, and murders that they had played over and over again in their minds.

Dungeons and Dragons has been heavily promoted in the Gifted Children Newsletter[7] and in the 1987 ''Gifted Child Today Catalog'' for its ''educational merit.'' In fact, D & D has been endorsed by the Association for Gifted-Creative Children because the game encourages the reading of Shakespeare, Tolkien, and Isaac Asimov.[8] A version of D & D specially adapted for use in schools has long been a staple of many Gifted-and-Talented programs across the country, although fortunately an increasing number of schools have wisely chosen to remove it from their classrooms.

It is a fact confirmed by onetime participants as well as by law-enforcement groups that certain Satanist, Wiccan, and other Neo-pagan groups seek to recruit new members from among the ranks of dedicated Fantasy Role Playing advocates. They are prime candidates for recruitment into these groups, for they are already familiar with most of the philosophy, ritual, symbolism, and practice of these religions.

The Ouija Board

Because the Ouija board is manufactured by Parker Brothers and sold in toy stores next to Monopoly and Scrabble, many people have assumed that it is merely a fascinating and mysterious toy. *Nothing could be further from the truth!*

The Ouija is a truly ancient device that has existed in many parts of the world for centuries. Third-century Rome and Egypt, ancient Greece, China as far back as 500 B.C., thirteenth-century A.D. Mongols, and even North American Indians all had a form of the Ouija for the express purpose of contacting the spirits.[9] In 1853 a French Spiritualist named M. Planchette invented a form of the board that used a little heart-shaped, three-legged platform with a pencil as the front leg. The device was called, not surprisingly, a "planchette."

The modern Ouija board is a fairly simple device in and of itself. It consists merely of a small planchette (minus the pencil) and a smooth board on which are printed the letters of the alphabet, the numbers 0 to 9, and the words "yes," "no," and "good-bye." In a photograph of the board dated 1935[10] it is interesting to note that the board has a left-facing crescent moon and star (known as the satanic crescent) adjacent to the word "No," and a five-pointed star inside a circle (reminiscent of the pentagram) in the bottom right-hand corner. They did away with the star in later versions.

The name "Ouija" is simply derived from the French "oui" ("yes") and the German "ja" ("yes"). So what we have here is the "Yes Yes" board.

"Yes" to *what* is a question worth serious consideration, especially since some occult traditions hold that demons and other undesirable entities cannot fully operate in a person's life unless explicitly invited or welcomed. "Yes Yes" certainly implies some form of welcome to me.

Taxing the Spirits?

Ouija boards became a national rage during the First and Second World Wars, when people desperately wanted to know the fate of their loved ones in battle. Spiritism has traditionally experienced revivals during times of war and other catastrophes. It also became fashionable among the ladies to employ the board as a parlor game during the early 1900's. That's all the ever-alert IRS needed. In 1920 they declared the board a game, and as such subject to taxation.[11]

But the simple fact is that *Ouija is NOT a neutral device. Nor is it a toy. It is a dangerous spiritistic tool designed to contact spirit beings and develop psychic abilities.*

During the occult revival of the 1960's the board again soared in popularity, to the point that in 1966 Parker Brothers bought the rights to the Ouija board and moved its production (intriguingly) to Salem, Massachusetts. They sold over two million boards the first year, outselling Parker Brothers' traditional all-time favorite, Monopoly.[12] The movie *The Exorcist* sparked a new flurry of interest in the board, primarily among girls aged 11 through 18 who were curious about what the Ouija really could do.[13] Over ten million Ouija boards have been sold, which means that potentially 20 million Americans or more have played with it.[14] And, since Shirley Mac-Laine has made the channeling routine popular once again, you can be sure that business has continued to be brisk.

Demons in Disguise

Despite the fact that the Ouija board is sold in virtually every toy store in America, even occultists are often not blithe about recommending its use. While some occultists do indeed swear by the device, Manly P. Hall, one of the world's foremost occult historians, says this about the Ouija board:

> The Ouija-board . . . driven from most of the civilized countries of the world, is a psychic toy that has contributed many tragedies to man's mortal state. Automatic writing (an advanced form of Ouija), a weird, fascinating pastime, may end in a wide variety of disasters. . . . He who listens too often to the whisperings of the "spirits" may find his angels to be demons in disguise . . . man . . . should leave alone these forces which may only lead to madness.[15]

The Donning International Encyclopedic Psychic Dictionary defines the Ouija and then adds:

> . . . a dangerous tool when used by one not well-grounded in psychic sciences

and knowledge of beforehand prepa-
ration; when used as a game for those
unfamiliar with psychic tuning it has
been known to draw the inferior entities to move the indicator; this inferior entity fools the user and can lead
to dangerous physical phenomena.[16]

Stoker Hunt, in his secular book *Ouija: The
Most Dangerous Game*, presents extensive and
sobering documentation and case histories dealing with the dangers of experimentation with
the Ouija board,[17] but then proceeds to give
instructions on how to use it if you still think you
really want to!

The Victims: Board to Tears

The September 30, 1986, edition of *Weekly World
News* reported that a 15-year-old in Belfast, Ire-
land, committed suicide shortly after the Ouija
board predicted his death before his sixteenth
birthday. "I've only got a short time to live, so I
might as well choose the time to die," he told
friends. They thought he was joking—until they
found him hanging in the churchyard.

An 11-year-old girl was told by the board that
she would be struck dead. She changed from an
outgoing and happy little girl to a terrified child
who was afraid to leave the house. Her grades
dropped to failing, she lost weight, and she
showed signs of paranoia until "eventually, after
a lot of visits, heartache and considerable ex-
pense, the psychiatrist was able to cure the child
of the dread that had scarred her youth."[18]

A 15-year-old girl working the board with her mother was instructed to murder her father so that her mother could marry a handsome young cowboy. She killed him. Despite the fact that the board had told them they would get away with the crime, both went to prison.[19]

A Christian child wrote to me from Union Lake, Michigan, to tell me that—

> A girl at school has a Ouija board. She was asking some girls at school to go to the graveyard and contact "ghosts." I said they were demonic, and I was ridiculed. I'm only in the sixth grade. So are they.

The Game's Up!

In April of 1987 I was invited by several mothers to testify at a school board meeting in Ontario, California, concerning the occult nature and dangers of the Ouija board. It seems that a certain sixth-grade teacher kept a Ouija board in his class for voluntary use during recess on rainy days. When a concerned mother requested removal of the board on the grounds that it was a dangerous occult tool, the teacher adamantly refused to remove the Ouija from his class and promptly consulted his attorney to make certain that "his civil rights were not being violated" by the outrageous request. After extensive publicity, the school board was eventually pressured into conducting public hearings. The teacher at this point generously decided to consider a compromise. He said he would be "willing to remove

the Ouija board from his classroom if the 'true
believers' would 'sign a pledge not to meddle
with the curriculum or classroom instruction of
any teacher... for purposes of propagating a
particular set of theological precepts.' "[20] His
opinion of the committee that temporarily sus-
pended the Ouija until a formal decision could be
made, and of the parents who questioned his wisdom, was quoted in the local paper as follows:

> ...A real dumb move...they're
> succumbing to the shouts and shrieks
> of these people....It's like waving a
> white flag in front of these Iranian
> fanatics dressed in Christian guise.[21]

Despite receiving over 96 pieces of documentation from concerned parents, teachers, police
officers, and ministers totaling more than 500
pages, plus dozens of other quotes and excerpts
from a wide range of sources (including para-
psychologists, psychiatrists, counselors, psychologists, and assorted occultists), the Ontario
School Board Committee was unable to come to
the conclusion that the Ouija board was either
occultic or potentially dangerous to the children.
The materials presented, we were told in their
written conclusions dated June 15, 1987, were
not "verified by empirical research data..." and
therefore "...the Committee does not make a
judgement on this issue."

My guess is that it was not "lack of empirical
evidence" that kept the Committee from declar-
ing the Ouija board occultic and dangerous (and

thereby banning it from their classrooms) but rather that, as reported by Marianne Aiken in the *Daily Report*, "Banning a Ouija board . . . would lead to a series of continuing demands for prohibition of other games or instructional material."

As one pro-Ouija mother warned in a statement to the trustees that may have been more revealing than she intended:

> . . . they [the anti-Ouija parents] might also seek to ban other occult equipment, studies and holidays. . . .[22]

If the game in question had been Bible Trivia, there would have been no question whatever concerning the teacher's alleged "violation of his First Amendment rights." The teacher defending his right to keep such a religiously biased game in his classroom would be laughed out of the hearings if he passionately proclaimed that "his rights as a teacher" were being violated because he had been asked to remove it! Nor would his students have been led in a discussion as to why they had been "cheated out of their freedom of choice."[23] Christian teachers and children have no choice concerning the open practice or discussion of their beliefs in the public school. The same rules should apply to Spiritualists, New Agers, and other occultists.

3

Pagan Playday

I was working on this chapter last night, Halloween, when the doorbell rang. I was greeted by an adorable bunch of little kids doing their level best to look like gruesome Witches and vampires. I bent down as I distributed apples and oranges in response to lusty cries of "trick or treat!"

"You kids want to know something?" I asked very softly.

"Yeah!" came a unanimous chorus.

"With the Lord Jesus there is no trick. He loves every one of you very much."

Several little faces beamed up at me through their ghoulish makeup. "That's neat!" exclaimed one little girl. "Yeah!" chimed in a few others.

"This is Jesus' night," I said. Why, I'm not really sure. I was poignantly aware of the fact that it is a night the devil has made a point of claiming for himself.

"No it's not!" snarled a hidden voice. "It's *Jason's* night!" A boy who was taller than the rest stepped out from the shadows. He was wearing the white hockey mask of "Jason," the demented, ghoulish killer in the movie *Friday the 13th* and was brandishing a very realistic-looking hatchet. I have to admit that the boy gave me a start, but I stood my ground and dropped a banana into his bag.

"No, 'Jason,' this is still Jesus' night!" I repeated. And indeed it is, even though it is most assuredly the night set aside for the glorification and worship of idols, false gods, Satan, and death. "The Son of God appeared for this purpose, that He might destroy the works of the devil!"[1]

"Jason" evidently resented the competition, however, for he ripped our mailbox right out of the ground and left his banana squished on the stair.

Church-Sponsored Horror

Most of us in the United States have grown up observing Halloween in one form or another. From the time we're in preschool we make drawings or cutouts of sinister black Witches—the haggier the better. We make paintings of gruesome black cats with gleaming, evil, orange eyes; we hang up smirking paper skeletons with dancing limbs; we glue together ghost and bat mobiles; and we design demoniacal faces for our pumpkins.

Even in the church, Halloween is a time of spooky fun and games. Any number of good, solid churches, ever mindful of their youth programs and ministries, will sponsor haunted houses designed to scare the wits out of the kids. In Bakersfield, California, Youth for Christ's Campus Life, a heavy-metal rock radio station, Pepsi, and Burger King are yearly sponsors of

"Scream in the Dark," an event held every night for about a week before Halloween. At least 20,000 people "brave the chilly corridors and dark passages" every year to face ghoulish figures, terrifying tunnels, and screams in the dark.[2]

The Lawndale Christian Church in Lawndale, California, offers discount coupons for "The House." The advertisement reads "You are entering at your own risk. Young children strongly recommended not to enter 'THE HOUSE.' Children under 12 must be accompanied by an adult. Persons with heart conditions, health problems or pregnant women are not allowed. . . ."

The warning is well-given. Terror can kill. When my husband was a teenager, the family next door to him lost their toddler one Halloween when the little one opened the door to trick-or-treaters. Their hideous appearance and shrieks so traumatized the child that he literally dropped dead on the spot.

Halloween has become a full-fledged national children's playday, but for hundreds of thousands of people in the Western world (and their numbers are growing steadily) Halloween is a sacred time, the ancient pagan festival of fire and death.

Ancient Origins

The origins and traditions of Halloween can be traced back thousands of years to the days of the ancient Celts and their priests, the Druids. The eve of October 31 marked the transition from summer into the darkness of winter. It

marked the beginning of the Celtic New Year.
The Feast of Samhain was a fearsome night, a
dreaded night, a night in which great bonfires
were lit to Samana the Lord of Death, the dark
Aryan god who was known as the Grim Reaper,
the leader of the ancestral ghosts.[3]

On this night the spirits of the dead rose up,
shivering with the coming cold of winter and
seeking the warmth and affection of the homes
they once inhabited. And even colder, darker
creatures filled the night: evil Witches flying
through the night,[4] hobgoblins, and evil pookas
that appeared in the form of hideous black horses.
Demons, fairies, and ghouls roamed about as the
doors of the burial *sidh*-mounds opened wide,[5]
allowing them free access to the world of living
men. These loathsome beings were usually not
in a particularly good mood by the time they
arrived and it was feared that unless these spirits
were appeased and soothed with offerings and
gifts they would wreak mischief and vengeance
by destroying crops, killing cattle, turning milk
sour, and generally making life miserable.

So it was that families offered what was most
precious to them: food—a "treat" which they
fervently hoped would be sufficient to offset any
"trick" which the ghostly blackmailers might
otherwise be tempted to inflict.

The ancient Celtic villagers realized, however,
that merely feeding the spirits might not be
enough to speed them on their way. So arose the
practice of dressing in masks and costumes:
Chosen villagers disguised themselves as the fell
creatures at large, mystically taking on their

attributes and powers. The "mummers," as they were called, cavorted from house to house collecting the ancient Celtic equivalent of protection money, and then romped the ghosts right out of town when they were through.

They carried a jack-o'-lantern to light their way—a turnip or potato with a fearful, demonic face carved into it which they hoped would duly impress, if not intimidate, the demons around them.

Spirited Communion

To modern Witches, who base many of their beliefs and practices on the Druidic religion, Halloween is one of the four greater Sabbats held during the year. It is the time of Harvest Celebration—that season in which the Great Goddess goes to sleep for the long winter months, giving way to the Horned God of Hunting and Death, who will rule until her return on the first of May. It is a time of ritual and for ridding oneself of personal weaknesses,[6] a time for feasting and joyful celebration. It is also a time for communing with the spirits of the dead.

An article in the *Los Angeles Times* (Saturday, October 31, 1987) features a story on a certain coven's celebration rituals during Halloween. The story describes the ritual and then tells us that it "will be repeated throughout the Southland today as Witches celebrate their most important holiday, Samhain, or Halloween, when they believe the veil between the worlds becomes thin, making visits with spirits possible." Some

Witches will use the Ouija board to contact the dead. Others will use a darkened scrying-mirror into which they stare until the faces of their beloved departed appear. Others may use a crystal ball or "sit quietly round the cauldron, gazing into the incense-smoke, talking of what they see and feel."[7]

Satanic Revels

While the Witches are spending the Halloween season tucking in their Goddess for her long winter sleep and frolicking in joyful communion with the spirits of the dead, there is another religious group which is equally serious about its Halloween celebrations: the Satanists. Halloween to them is a more sinister and direct celebration of death and Satan.

As is the case among the Witches, different "denominations" of Satanists have their own peculiar traditions, beliefs, and practices on this night. For some of them Satan is not a real, specific entity, but rather the personification of evil resident within all men, a "dark hidden force in nature responsible for the workings of earthly affairs. . . ."[8]

Other Satanists however—cult Satanists—understand that Satan is very real indeed. To them the sacrifices he demands are not symbolic at all.[9] They believe that the blood sacrifice of innocence which Satan demands as the ultimate blasphemy and sign of devotion to himself must be very literal indeed.

The rituals of some of these satanic cults are

unspeakably vicious and brutal, as Lauren Stratford in her powerful and important book *Satan's Underground* relates. One of the most horrible practices of the particular satanic cult which victimized her for many years was the ritual slaughter of an infant or very young child and an adult female on the night of Halloween. Although not all Satanist groups participate in activities of this kind, some certainly do.

The night of Halloween is also a propitious time for some Satanists to contact the spirits of the dead. Their rituals of necromancy often go far beyond that of the Witches and mediums in the horror and perversion in which these people specialize. After the sacrifices the group might transfer to a solitary graveyard. A casket is unearthed and the lid pried open. Sometimes this ritual will take place in a mortuary rather than a cemetery. Ritual words are spoken to cast out "the spirit of death" and to invoke into the decaying body the "spirit of life," which is then adjured to answer any question the high priest puts to it. Victims have told of being placed inside the coffin in a ritual "embracing of death."

Imitators of God

So . . . should your family participate in the traditional Halloween celebrations? Absolutely . . . *if* you and/or your children are Witches, Satanists, Humanists, atheists, or anything other than born-again Christians (or Orthodox Jews). For a true Christian to participate in the ancient trappings of Halloween is as incongruous as for a committed cult Satanist coming from a blood sacrifice on Christmas Eve to set up a crèche in his living room and sing "Silent Night, Holy Night" with heartfelt, sincere devotion to Baby Jesus.

"But it's only for one night!" you cry. "It's only in fun for the children!" If this is how you feel, then you need to understand what the Word of God says to you:

> Learn not the way of the heathen! (Jeremiah 10:2 KJV). Do not be bound together with unbelievers; for what partnership have righteousness and lawlessness, or what fellowship has light with darkness? Or what harmony has Christ with Belial, or what has a believer in common with an unbeliever? Or what agreement has the temple of God with idols? For we are the temple of the living God; just as God said, "I will dwell in them and walk among them; and I will be their God, and they shall be My people. Therefore, come out from their midst and be separate," says the Lord. "And do not touch what is unclean" (2 Corinthians 6:14-17).

Halloween is a day in which virtually everything that God has called *abomination* is glorified.[10] We have no business participating in that at any time, much less in the name of "fun."

Creative Alternatives

There are any number of creative alternatives that can be provided for children on Halloween without participating in the ancient religious traditions of the Witches and Satanists.

I've heard Mike Warnke suggest that parents and churches hold costume parties and have the kids come as Bible heroes. (And don't just make it "Bible characters" in general. After all, Satan, Baal, Belial, Beelzebul and Moloch are mentioned in there!) Some groups have set up bowling or ice-skating parties.

Some families view the occasion as a witnessing opportunity, and hand out gospel tracts along with the treats. Some churches are now sponsoring "Bible Houses," in which the kids go through and hear different Bible stories read or acted out—a godly alternative to the haunted-house routine!

Other Christian families choose to spend the night remembering the saints who have gone to be with the Lord during the year. A saint, according to the Bible, is *anyone* who has believed in the Lord Jesus Christ as his personal Messiah. Perhaps you could spend this night talking about the martyrs who were willing to die rather than compromise their belief in the Lord Jesus Christ.

Christian parents can also make a difference in the way the schools which their children attend celebrate Halloween. *The Eagle's Forum* of Fall 1987 reported a story about parents in Colorado who have protested the traditional celebration of Halloween in several public schools, including at least one elementary school, on the grounds that it is a "high holy day in the satanic religion, and as such is an inappropriate holiday for schoolchildren."[11] Since God and Jesus have been banned from Christmas and Easter and Thanksgiving celebrations in most of our schools, why should the Witches and Satanists get free promotion on Halloween from those same institutions?

One thing that Halloween should *not* be for the Christian is a time of fear. It should be a time to rejoice in the fact that "the Son of God appeared for this purpose, that He might destroy the works of the devil" (1 John 3:8)! Spend at least part of this night worshiping God by singing hymns. Above all, spend time in prayer and intercession for the children.

It is tragic that many people in the church have forgotten that "God has not given us a spirit of fear, but of power and of love and of a sound mind" (from 2 Timothy 1:7 KJV), and that includes on Halloween!

> You were formerly darkness, but now you are light in the Lord; walk as children of light . . . and do not participate in the unfruitful deeds of darkness, but instead even expose them (Ephesians 5:8,11).

Notes

Introduction

1. Religious News Service, "Parapsychology More Popular," the *Bakersfield Californian*, Dec. 27, 1986, p. C1. This was a 1981 Gallup Poll. A poll in 1986 by *USA Weekend* gave the same results ("Looking into the Beyond," *USA Weekend, Houston Post*, Jan. 9-11, 1987, p. 4).
2. Andrew Greeley, "Mysticism Goes Mainstream," *American Health*, Feb. 1987, pp. 47-55.

Chapter 1—The War for Your Child's Mind

1. Robert Maynard Hutchins, ed., "On Poetics," *Great Books of the Western World*, vol. 9, Aristotle: II (Encyclopedia Britannica, Inc., 1980), pp. 682, 1448b.
2. Dr. David Pearl, Ph.D., *Television and Behavior: Ten Years of Scientific Progress and Implications for the Eighties*, vol. 1: Summary Report (Rockville, MD: U.S. Dept. of Health and Human Services, National Institute of Mental Health [5600 Fishers Lane, Rockville, MD 20857], 1982).
3. Eugene H. Methvin, "TV Violence: The Shocking New Evidence," *Reader's Digest*, Jan. 1983, p. 50.
4. For further reading on the significance of the rainbow and the New Age Movement, see Constance Cumbey, *The Hidden Dangers of the Rainbow* (Huntington House, 1983).
5. Moon Dreamers, "My Little Pony 'N Friends," from program viewed Oct. 18, 1987.
6. "He-Man and the Masters of the Universe," on program I watched Oct. 23, 1984.
7. Barbara G. Walker, *The Woman's Encyclopedia of Myths and Secrets* (San Francisco, CA: Harper and Row Publishers, 1983), p. 838.
8. Manly P. Hall, *The Secret Teachings of All Ages: An Encyclopedic Outline of Masonic, Hermetic, Qabbalistic and Rosicrucian Symbolical Philosophy* (Los Angeles, CA: The Philosophical Research Society, Inc., 1977), p. XCII.
9. *New Webster's Dictionary of the English Language*, Deluxe Encyclopedic ed. (Delair Publishing Co., 1981), p. 15.
10. Richard Cavendish, ed., *Man, Myth and Magic*, vol. 21 (New York: Marshall Cavendish Corp., 1970), p. 2910.
11. *The Unicorn King and Other Stories*, a She-Ra videotape, Filmation/Magic Window, Mattel, Inc., 1985.
12. Boris Matthews, trans., *The Herder Symbol Dictionary: Symbols from Art, Archaeology, Mythology, Literature, and Religion* (Wilmette, IL: Chiron Publications, 1986), p. 52.
13. Dale Pollock, *Skywalking: The Life and Films of George Lucas* (New York: Harmony Books, 1983), p. 2.
14. Ibid., p. 144.
15. Ibid., p. 139.
16. Ibid., p. 140.
17. Ibid.
18. Sue Cornwell and Mike Kott, *The Official Price Guide to Star Trek and Star Wars Collectibles* (New York: Random House, Inc., published by The House of Collectibles, 1986).
19. "Film and Television," *Chicago Tribune*, Apr. 8, 1982.

20. Richard Cavendish, *The Black Arts* (Capricorn Books Edition, 1968), p. 242.
21. Matthew 15:22; 17:14-18; Mark 9:17-26; Luke 9:38-42.
22. Cheryl Simon, "The Joy of Toys: The Playthings of Children Reflect the Values and Concerns of Society," *Washington Post Health*, Dec. 25, 1985, p. 10.
23. Thomas Radecki, M.D., "The TV War on Children: Savagery Is Fair and Fun in Television's Kid Cartoons," *The Christian Reader*, July/Aug. 1986, p. 16.
24. "T.V.'s Influence on Kids Is More than We Thought," *Long Beach Press-Telegram* from *New York Daily News*, Mar. 4, 1989.
25. Ibid.
26. Michael R. Kelley, *A Parents' Guide to Television: Making the Most of It*, Wiley Parent Education Series (John Wiley and Sons, Inc., 1983), p. 42
27. Those children's books listed and others are available through your local Christian bookstore.
28. Deborah Smith, *The Faithful's Journey Through Fairy Land*, (1989), pp. 9-10.

Chapter 2—"Pure" Fantasy?

1. Mitchell Fink, "Co-Creator of Dungeons and Dragons Defends Game's Violence," *Los Angeles Herald Examiner*, Sept. 14, 1985.
2. Gary Gygax, *Advanced Dungeons and Dragons: Player's Handbook*, 1978, p. 7.
3. Ibid.
4. Ibid., p. 20.
5. Ibid., p. 25.
6. Billy Bowles, "A Deadly Game?" *Detroit Free Press*, Michigan, Oct. 13, 1985.
7. Kristine K. Thompson, "Role-Playing Games: Expect the Unexpected," *Gifted Children Newsletter*, vol. 5, no. 2, Feb. 1984.
8. Jerry Adler with Shawn Doherty, "Kids: The Deadliest Game?" *Newsweek*, Sept. 9, 1985.
9. Stoker Hunt, *Ouija: The Most Dangerous Game* (New York: Barnes and Noble Books, a division of Harper and Row Publishers, 1985), p. 4.
10. James P. Johnson, *American Heritage Magazine*, Feb./Mar. 1983, p. 27.
11. Hunt, *Ouija*, p. 6.
12. Ibid.
13. Dr. Kurt Koch, *Occult A B C* (Kregel Publications, 1978), p. 154.
14. John Godwin, *Occult America* (New York: Doubleday and Co., Inc., 1972), p. 271.
15. Manly P. Hall, *Questions and Answers—Fundamentals of the Esoteric Sciences* (Los Angeles, CA: The Philosophical Research Society, Inc., 1979), pp. 95-96.
16. June G. Bletzer, *The Donning International Encyclopedic Psychic Dictionary* (Norfolk/Virginia Beach: The Donning Co., 1986), p. 447.
17. In light of warnings such as these, and there are dozens of them I could have listed, it is especially distressing to find well-respected

"men of the cloth" advocating use of the Ouija. In his book *The Christian and the Supernatural* Episcopal priest and Jungian psychologist Morton Kelsey openly encourages Christians to develop occult abilities. He informs us on pages 71-72 that "Another way of coming into contact with the realm which mediums reach is by using a Ouija board, one of the most popular games in America.... Whether the answers come from one's own unconscious or from outside, they often supply amazing insights and even information."

His one word of caution: "It is unfortunate ... that so many people make a game of encountering the psychic realm." Evidently he would like us to be *serious* about our occult development! A shocking perspective from one who should know better, but then again, Rev. Kelsey believes that Jesus was the greatest *shaman* that ever lived (Morton Kelsey, *Dreams: A Way to Listen to God*, p. 23), so I suppose the rest should not come as a major surprise.

18. Hunt, *Ouija*, p. 13.
19. Ibid., p. 14.
20. Bob Muir, *Progress Bulletin* (Ontario, CA), Feb. 27, 1987.
21. Ibid., Mar. 13, 1987.
22. Ibid., Feb. 27, 1987.
23. Ibid., Mar. 14, 1987.

Chapter 3—Pagan Playday

1. 1 John 3:8.
2. Connie Swart, "Event Still a Scream," the *Bakersfield Californian*, October 16, 1987, F13.
3. Walker, *The Woman's Encyclopedia of Myths*, p. 372.
4. *Encyclopedia of Witchcraft and Demonology* (London: Octopus Books Ltd., 1974), p. 166. Introduction by Hans Holzer.
5. Janet and Stewart Farrar, *A Witches Bible*, vol. 1, the Sabbats (New York: Magickal Childe Publishing, Inc., 1981, 1984), p. 122.
6. Raymond Buckland, *Buckland's Complete Book of Witchcraft* (Minneapolis: Llewellyn Publications, 1986), p. 68.
7. Farrar and Farrar, *A Witches Bible*, vol 1, the Sabbats, p. 135.
8. Anton Szandor LaVey, *The Satanic Bible* (New York: Avon Books, 1969), p. v of introduction.
9. Anton LaVey clarifies his position on human sacrifice on page 88 of his *Satanic Bible*, in which he says: "Symbolically, the victim is destroyed through the working of a hex or curse, which in turn leads to the physical, mental or emotional destruction of the 'sacrifice' in ways and means not attributable to the magician. The only time a Satanist would perform a human sacrifice would be if it were to serve a two-fold purpose; that being to release the magician's wrath in the throwing of a curse, and more important, to dispose of a totally obnoxious and deserving individual."
10. Deuteronomy 18:9-14.
11. Rebecca Jones, "Halloween Parade Off," *The Eagle Forum*, vol. 8, no. 4, Fall 1987, p. 17.